The Three Silly Cowboys

Written by Deb Eaton
Illustrated by Jared Lee

Once upon a time,
there were three cowboys.

They liked to ride, and rope, and
fix fences.

They worked hard all day long.

"I'm sleepy," said the first cowboy.

"I'm sleepy, too," said the second cowboy.

"YAWN!" said the third cowboy.

So all three of them sat down by a tree
to take a nap.

When they woke up, they could not stand up.

All their feet looked the same.

"I need help," said the first cowboy.

"I need help, too," said the second cowboy.

"HELP!" yelled the third cowboy.

A young farmer came by.

"I can help you," he said.

"Yes, please," said the first cowboy.

"Oh, yes," said the second cowboy.

"YES!" yelled the third cowboy.

"OK," said the farmer.
"I will use a big feather."

TICKLE-TICKLE went the feather.

"He, he, he!" said the first cowboy.

"Those are *your* feet," the young farmer said.

TICKLE-TICKLE went the feather.

"He, he, he!" said the second cowboy.

"Those are your feet," the young
farmer said.

TICKLE-TICKLE went the feather.

"He, he, he!" said the third cowboy.

"And those are *your* feet," the young farmer said.

"Thanks," said the first cowboy.

"Thanks," said the second cowboy.

"Thank you very much," yelled the
third cowboy.

"You're welcome," the young
farmer said.